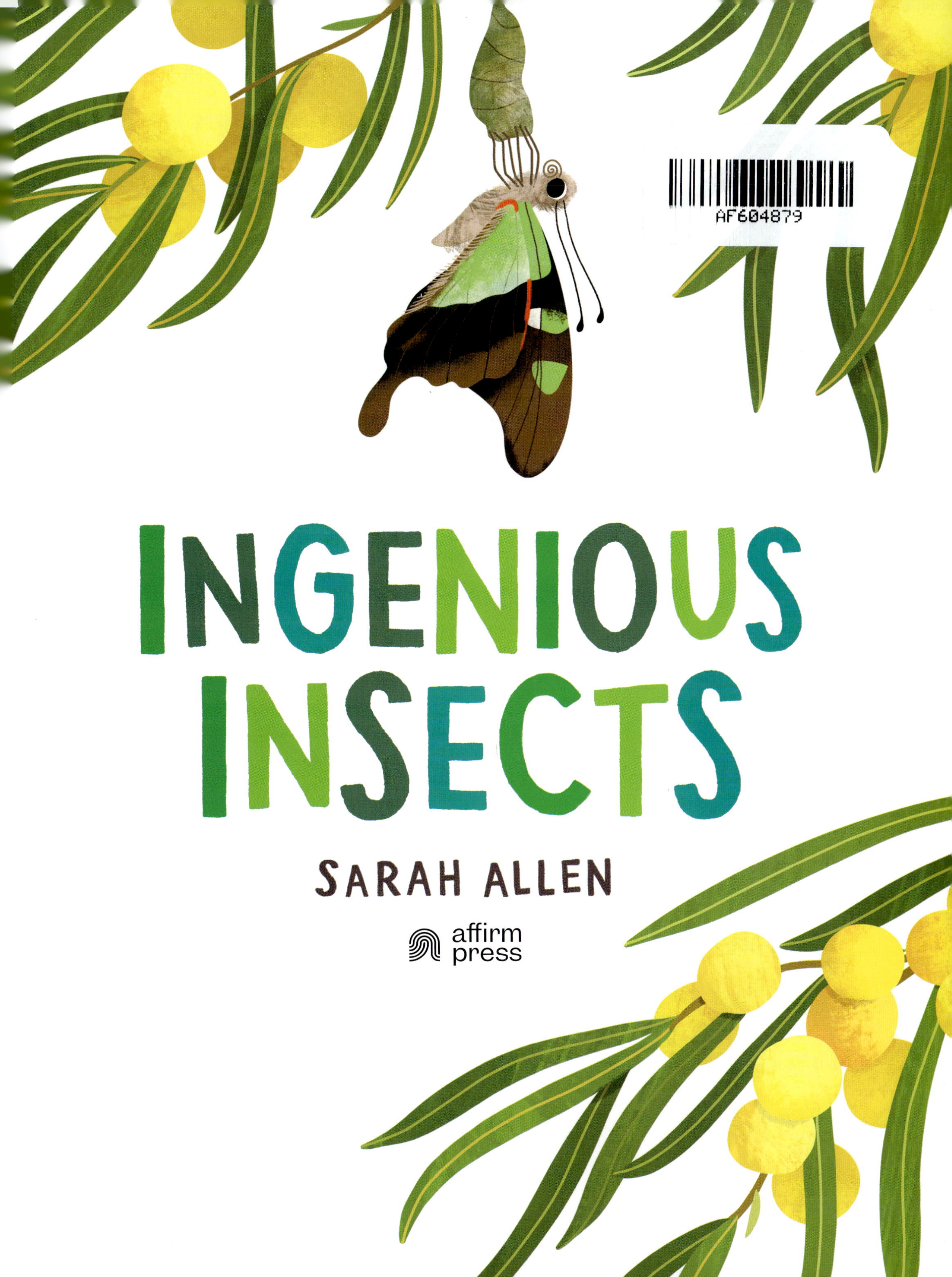

INGENIOUS INSECTS

SARAH ALLEN

affirm press

Yellow Admiral
Vanessa itea
Imperial Jezebel
Delias harpalyce
Common Grass Yellow
Eurema hecabe

Macleay's Swallowtail
Graphium macleayanum
Blue Triangle
Graphium choredon

Noisy cicadas
chirp summer songs.

Greengrocer Cicada
Cyclochila australasiae

Dragonflies hover above creeks and ponds.

Fiery Skimmer Dragonfly
Orthetrum villosovittatum

Grasshoppers leap in the warmth of the sun.

Thermocolour Skyhopper
Kosciuscola tristis

Feasting on flowers,
hoverflies hum.

Rhinoceros beetles battle and fight.

Sneaky stick insects hide in plain sight.

Margin-winged Stick Insect
Ctenomorpha marginipennis

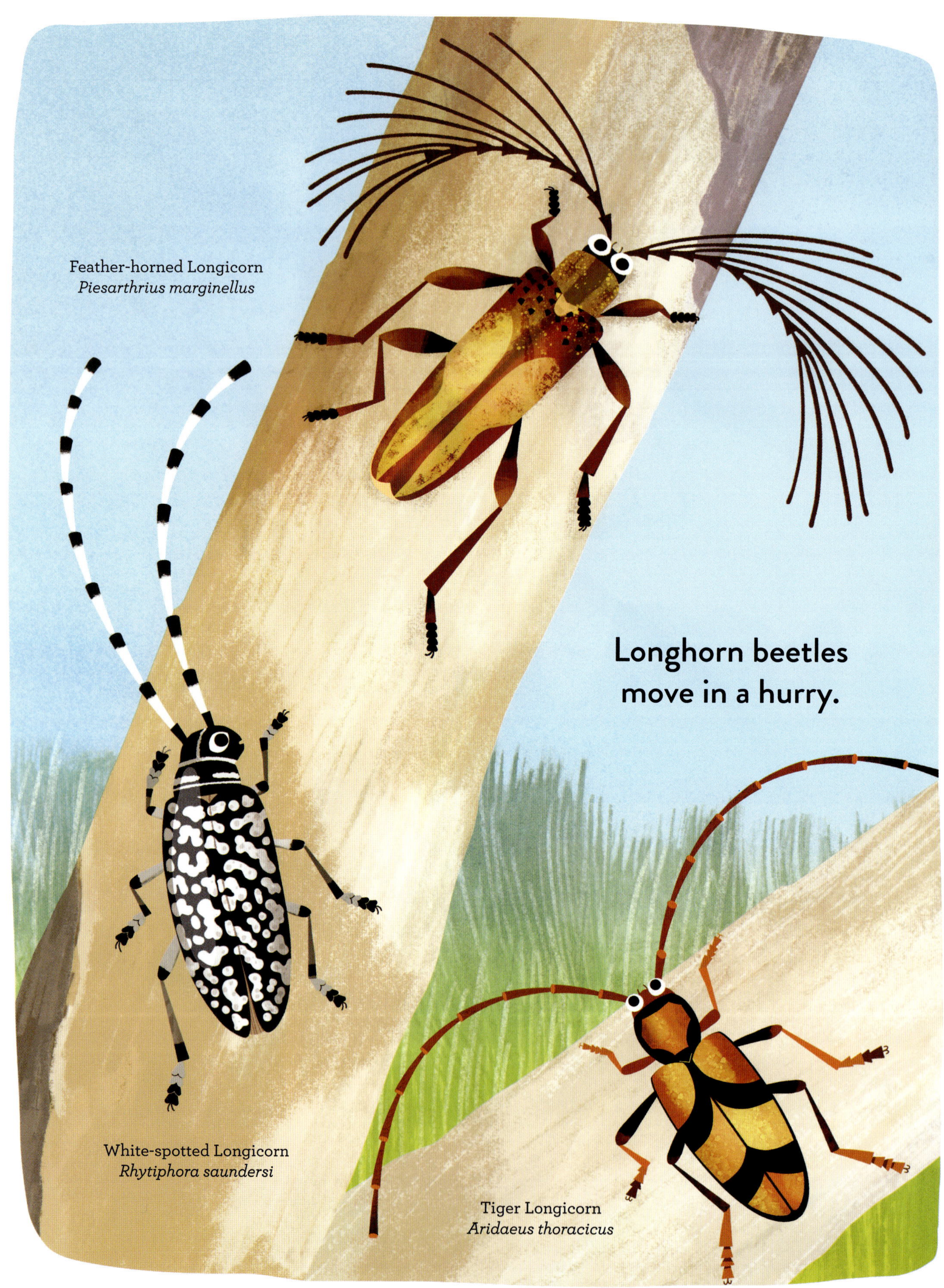

Longhorn beetles move in a hurry.

Red Spotted Jewel Beetle
Stigmodera cancellata
Shiny jewel beetles
shimmer and scurry.
Scalaris Jewel Beetle
Castiarina scalaris

Bee colonies make sugary food.

Burrowing bees dig holes
for their brood.
Common Blue-banded Bee
Amegilla cingulata

Under the leaves,
earwigs forage at night.

Fireflies flash their signals of light.

Blue Mountains Firefly
Atyphella lychnus

Butterflies drink sweet nectar from flowers.

Termites take flight after summer rain showers.

Tree Termite
Nasutitermes walkeri

Owlflies hover and dive on their prey.

Australian Common Owlfly
Suhpalacsa subtrahens

Lacewings keep
hungry aphids away.

A fast praying mantis hunts snacks with ease.

Katydids sway in the cool autumn breeze.

Gum Leaf Katydid
Terpandrus horridus

In winter months, few bugs buzz around.
Ant colonies stay warm underground.

Giant Meat Ant
Iridomyrmex purpureus

Ladybirds huddle and sleep until spring.

Common Spotted Ladybird
Harmonia conformis

Tiny eggs hatch into wriggling things.

Bottlebrush Sawfly
Pterygophorus cinctus

Beetle nymphs grow,
moult and change shape.

Long-nosed Lycid Beetle
Porrostoma rhipidius

Caterpillars get ready and quietly wait.

Emperor Gum Moth Caterpillar
Opodiphthera eucalypti

Forest Splendid Ghost Moth
Aenetus eximia
Emperor Gum Moth
Opodiphthera eucalypti
Grapevine Hawk Moth
Hippotion celerio
Bogong Moth
Agrotis infusa

Hercules Moth
Coscinocera hercules
Clara's Satin Moth
Thalaina clara
Four-Spot Anthelid
Anthela guenei

SIX-LEGGED SUPERHEROES

Insects have been around for hundreds of millions of years – they were here WAY before the dinosaurs. There are tens of thousands of insect species in Australia, and many more are still waiting to be discovered. We need insects to help us grow food and to keep our ecosystems healthy. Insects support all life on Earth.

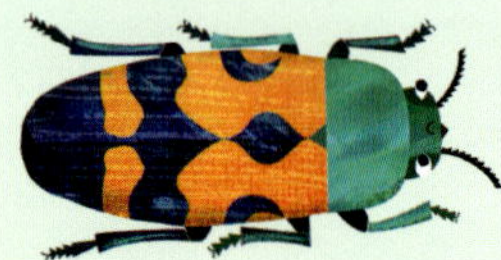

JEWEL BEETLES

are known for their marvellous, metallic colours. Like most beetles, they have a pair of hardened wings that protect their delicate flying wings underneath.

LADY BEETLES

are known for their distinctive spots but also come in many other colours and patterns. They are predators and help keep other insect species like aphids in check, maintaining a balanced ecosystem.

DIGGER BEES

do not live in a colony or make honey! Instead of living in a hive, females live mostly alone and dig a small hole for their eggs. Australia has many native bee species; most of them build their nests in the ground.

MEAT ANTS

are incredible at working together in enormous colonies. Meat ants don't sting, but they have impressive mandibles that they use to carry large pieces of food and defend themselves from intruders!

LONGHORN BEETLES

get their name from their antennae, which can be longer than their bodies! The largest insect in the world is a longhorn beetle: the Titan Beetle, which can grow to almost 18 cm long!

NET-WINGED BEETLES

have larvae that live in decaying wood and are part of nature's clean-up crew. They help to break down dead trees and recycle nutrients by eating them and pooping them out! The adults are brightly coloured, warning predators away.

NATIVE STINGLESS BEES

collect nectar and pollen from flowers, turn it into honey and store it in their waxy nest. Unlike European honey bees, native stingless bees only make enough honey for themselves. These bee species are often very small and can be mistaken for flies or other tiny insects.

FIREFLIES

are actually beetles and not flies at all! Their blinky bottoms are lit up through a chemical reaction in their bodies that creates bioluminescence.

RHINOCEROS BEETLES

are super strong for their size and are able to lift many hundred times their own body weight. Using their horns, males wrestle each other to win the right to mate with a female.

TERMITES

nest in mounds that they build in the ground or in trees. hen the time comes to start new colonies, some termites y out of their nest in a gentle fluttering swarm. Termites are vital for breaking down dead and decaying wood and enriching the soil with nutrients.

SAWFLIES

are relatives of wasps, bees and ants. They have famous larvae, often called 'spitfires', which feed in a group, stripping leaves down to their skeletons. If the group of larvae detect a threat, they wiggle their bottoms in the air all at the same time! Adult sawflies are pollinators of flowering plants.

PRAYING MANTISES

are brilliant hunters. They stay very still, waiting for their prey to come close, then pounce with their 'raptorial' front legs to catch super-fast insects. Mantises have developed ways to startle their predators, including making weird sounds and raising their wings or arms to flash surprising colours.

STICK INSECTS

are masters of disguise. They have evolved to look like sticks and leaves in their surroundings, making it difficult for their predators to detect them. Stick insects are herbivores; they eat the leaves of plants, shrubs and trees.

DRAGONFLIES

are expert fliers that can hover, fly backwards and change direction with spectacular speed and precision. They have large, complex eyes that help them hunt flying insects in mid-air. Young dragonfly 'nymphs' live in water until they crawl out onto pond plants to transform into adults and spread their new wings.

LACEWINGS

are dainty-looking insects with long, delicate wings. Lacewings are predators that can help gardeners keep other insect populations in check. Young lacewings are called 'ant lions'. They live at the bottom of small, sandy pits, waiting for ants to fall in so they can eat them.

OWLFLIES

get their name from their large, bulging eyes. They are frequently mistaken for dragonflies because of their four separated wings, but owlflies have long antennae with clubbed ends while dragonflies have very short antennae that are hard to spot!

HOVERFLIES

might look and act like bees but are a type of fly. There are thousands of amazing fly species in Australia. By buzzing between flowers as they feed, hoverflies are excellent pollinators, and some of them are predators too! Hoverflies, and in fact all flies, have two wings, while bees and most other insects have four.

KATYDIDS

often look so much like leaves that they can sit in plain view and avoid being detected by predators! Gum Leaf Katydids lay eggs that look like plant seeds, often in a row along leaves or stems. Many male katydids can sing chirpy songs by rubbing their wings together.

GRASSHOPPERS

have long, springy legs that they use to bound out of the way of hungry predators. Many grasshoppers make a noise using their back legs but some are silent. Thermocolour Skyhoppers change their body colour from black to turquoise blue depending on the temperature. They can only be found on the highest peaks of Australia's highest mountains.

CICADAS

are some of the noisiest insects on the planet! The loud sound of males calling for females in summer is an amazing feat that they accomplish by squeezing their tummies. Cicadas have five eyes: two big eyes and three small ones! The central three jewel-like eyes help to detect overhead predators.

BUTTERFLY CATERPILLARS

munch on leaves out in the open all day long, so they need to be well defended from predators. They can be spectacularly spiny, amazingly camouflaged and can even whistle and squeak! When it's time to transform, they make a chrysalis and emerge as an adult butterfly.

EARWIGS

have special body parts called 'cerci' located at their rear ends. They use these to capture prey and to help fold and unfold their wings. Mother earwigs keep their babies close. They care for their eggs and young nymphs until they can fend for themselves.

MOTH CATERPILLARS

also have clever ways to protect themselves, including spiky hairs that sting predators. Case moth caterpillars hang around in little brown tubes that are sometimes decorated with sticks. Wood moth and ghost moth caterpillars can spend years inside the wood of trees.

BUTTERFLY ADULTS

have wings covered in tiny scales that make amazing colours and patterns. Most butterflies like to warm up in the sun and fly in the daytime. Butterflies have a drinking straw called a 'proboscis' instead of a mouth, and they have their tastebuds on their feet!

Dedicated to Mum and Dad.

With special thanks to Dr Kate Umbers.

First published in Australia in 2024 by Affirm Press,
a Simon & Schuster (Australia) Pty Limited company
This edition published in 2025.
Bunurong/Boon Wurrung Country
28 Thistlethwaite Street, South Melbourne VIC 3205
Affirm Press is located on the unceded land of the Bunurong/Boon Wurrung peoples of the Kulin Nation.
Affirm Press pays respect to their Elders past and present.
AFFIRM PRESS and design are trademarks of Affirm Press Pty Ltd, Inc.,
used under licence by Simon & Schuster, LLC.
10 9 8 7 6 5 4 3 2 1

9781761820083 (paperback)
Cover and internal design by Kirby Armstrong
Printed and bound in China by RR Donnelley Asia

MOTH ADULTS

also have large wings and can be as colourful as butterflies. Most moths are active at night and have fuzzy bodies. Some male moths have spectacular feathery antennae that can detect smells from great distances.